50 Mediterranean Diet Recipes for Home

By: Kelly Johnson

Table of Contents

- Greek Salad with Feta and Olives
- Baked Salmon with Lemon and Dill
- Quinoa Tabbouleh with Fresh Herbs
- Grilled Eggplant with Tahini Sauce
- Mediterranean Chickpea Salad
- Stuffed Bell Peppers with Quinoa and Vegetables
- Hummus with Fresh Vegetables
- Spinach and Feta Pie (Spanakopita)
- Greek Yogurt with Honey and Walnuts
- Grilled Chicken with Tzatziki Sauce
- Roasted Red Pepper Hummus
- Falafel with Tahini Sauce
- Tomato and Cucumber Salad with Olive Oil
- Shrimp Saganaki with Feta
- Grilled Zucchini with Lemon and Garlic
- Whole Wheat Pita Bread with Olive Tapenade
- Lentil Soup with Lemon and Spinach
- Stuffed Grape Leaves (Dolmades)
- Couscous with Roasted Vegetables
- Grilled Swordfish with Capers and Olive Oil
- Roasted Eggplant Dip (Baba Ganoush)
- Chicken Souvlaki with Tzatziki
- Roasted Cauliflower with Lemon and Garlic
- Mediterranean Tuna Salad
- Chickpea and Spinach Stew
- Whole Wheat Pasta with Pesto and Tomatoes
- Grilled Halloumi Cheese with Tomato
- Braised Artichokes with Garlic and Herbs
- Caprese Salad with Fresh Mozzarella
- Sardines with Lemon and Olive Oil

- Roasted Beet Salad with Feta
- Grilled Octopus with Olive Oil and Herbs
- Lemon Orzo Salad with Feta and Olives
- Roasted Bell Peppers with Anchovies
- Ratatouille with Fresh Herbs
- Bulgur Wheat Salad with Pomegranate Seeds
- Baked Cod with Tomatoes and Olives
- Greek Lentil Salad with Red Wine Vinegar
- Zucchini Fritters with Feta
- Roasted Garlic and Herb Chicken
- Cucumber Yogurt Soup
- Baked Falafel with Tzatziki
- Olive Oil and Lemon Marinated Artichokes
- Grilled Vegetable Skewers with Halloumi
- Mediterranean Stuffed Eggplant
- Tomato and Feta Salad with Fresh Herbs
- Baked Sea Bass with Lemon and Capers
- Quinoa and Avocado Salad with Olive Oil
- Spinach Salad with Feta and Walnuts
- Mediterranean Lentil Soup

Greek Salad with Feta and Olives

Ingredients:

- 4 cups chopped cucumbers
- 2 cups cherry tomatoes, halved
- 1 red onion, thinly sliced
- 1 cup Kalamata olives, pitted
- 1 cup feta cheese, crumbled
- 1/4 cup olive oil
- 2 tablespoons red wine vinegar
- 1 teaspoon dried oregano
- Salt and pepper to taste

Instructions:

1. In a large bowl, combine cucumbers, cherry tomatoes, red onion, olives, and feta cheese.
2. In a small bowl, whisk together olive oil, red wine vinegar, oregano, salt, and pepper.
3. Drizzle the dressing over the salad and toss gently to combine.

Baked Salmon with Lemon and Dill

Ingredients:

- 4 salmon fillets
- 2 tablespoons olive oil
- 2 tablespoons fresh lemon juice
- 1 lemon, sliced
- 2 tablespoons fresh dill, chopped (or 1 tablespoon dried dill)
- Salt and pepper to taste

Instructions:

1. Preheat the oven to 375°F (190°C).
2. Place salmon fillets in a baking dish. Drizzle with olive oil and lemon juice, then season with salt, pepper, and dill.
3. Top each fillet with lemon slices. Bake for 15-20 minutes, or until the salmon is cooked through and flakes easily with a fork.

Quinoa Tabbouleh with Fresh Herbs

Ingredients:

- 1 cup quinoa, rinsed and drained
- 2 cups water
- 1 cup parsley, finely chopped
- 1/2 cup mint leaves, finely chopped
- 1 cup cherry tomatoes, diced
- 1 cucumber, diced
- 1/4 cup olive oil
- 2 tablespoons lemon juice
- Salt and pepper to taste

Instructions:

1. In a pot, bring water to a boil. Add quinoa, reduce heat, cover, and simmer for about 15 minutes or until the quinoa is cooked. Let it cool.
2. In a large bowl, combine cooked quinoa, parsley, mint, cherry tomatoes, and cucumber.
3. In a small bowl, whisk together olive oil, lemon juice, salt, and pepper. Drizzle over the salad and toss gently to combine.

Grilled Eggplant with Tahini Sauce

Ingredients:

- 2 medium eggplants, sliced into 1/2-inch rounds
- 1/4 cup olive oil
- Salt and pepper to taste
- 1/2 cup tahini
- 2 tablespoons lemon juice
- 2 cloves garlic, minced
- Water (as needed for consistency)
- Fresh parsley, chopped (for garnish)

Instructions:

1. Preheat the grill to medium-high heat. Brush eggplant slices with olive oil and season with salt and pepper.
2. Grill the eggplant for about 4-5 minutes on each side until tender and charred.
3. In a bowl, mix tahini, lemon juice, garlic, salt, and enough water to achieve a pourable consistency. Drizzle over the grilled eggplant and garnish with parsley.

Mediterranean Chickpea Salad

Ingredients:

- 1 can chickpeas, rinsed and drained
- 1 cucumber, diced
- 1 cup cherry tomatoes, halved
- 1/4 cup red onion, finely chopped
- 1/4 cup parsley, chopped
- 1/4 cup olive oil
- 2 tablespoons lemon juice
- Salt and pepper to taste

Instructions:

1. In a large bowl, combine chickpeas, cucumber, cherry tomatoes, red onion, and parsley.
2. In a small bowl, whisk together olive oil, lemon juice, salt, and pepper. Pour over the salad and toss to combine.

Stuffed Bell Peppers with Quinoa and Vegetables

Ingredients:

- 4 bell peppers, halved and seeds removed
- 1 cup cooked quinoa
- 1 cup diced tomatoes (canned or fresh)
- 1 zucchini, diced
- 1/2 cup corn (fresh or frozen)
- 1 teaspoon cumin
- 1 teaspoon paprika
- Salt and pepper to taste
- 1 cup shredded cheese (optional)

Instructions:

1. Preheat the oven to 375°F (190°C). In a large bowl, combine quinoa, tomatoes, zucchini, corn, cumin, paprika, salt, and pepper.
2. Fill each bell pepper half with the quinoa mixture and place in a baking dish. If using, sprinkle cheese on top.
3. Bake for 25-30 minutes, or until the peppers are tender.

Hummus with Fresh Vegetables

Ingredients:

- 1 can chickpeas, rinsed and drained
- 1/4 cup tahini
- 2 tablespoons olive oil
- 2 tablespoons lemon juice
- 1 clove garlic, minced
- Salt to taste
- Fresh vegetables (carrots, cucumbers, bell peppers, etc.) for dipping

Instructions:

1. In a food processor, combine chickpeas, tahini, olive oil, lemon juice, garlic, and salt. Blend until smooth, adding water if necessary for desired consistency.
2. Serve hummus with a platter of fresh vegetables for dipping.

Enjoy these delicious Mediterranean recipes that are not only healthy but also packed with flavor!

Spinach and Feta Pie (Spanakopita)

Ingredients:

- 1 pound fresh spinach, washed and chopped
- 1 cup feta cheese, crumbled
- 1/2 cup ricotta cheese
- 1 onion, finely chopped
- 2 cloves garlic, minced
- 1/4 cup fresh dill, chopped (or 1 tablespoon dried dill)
- 1 package phyllo pastry (about 16 sheets)
- 1/2 cup olive oil
- Salt and pepper to taste

Instructions:

1. Preheat the oven to 375°F (190°C). In a skillet, heat olive oil over medium heat. Sauté onion and garlic until soft.
2. Add spinach and cook until wilted. Remove from heat and let cool. Stir in feta, ricotta, dill, salt, and pepper.
3. Brush a baking dish with olive oil and layer 4 sheets of phyllo, brushing each with olive oil. Spread a portion of the spinach mixture over the phyllo.
4. Repeat layering phyllo and filling until all is used, finishing with phyllo. Brush the top with olive oil and score into squares.
5. Bake for 30-35 minutes, or until golden brown. Let cool slightly before serving.

Greek Yogurt with Honey and Walnuts

Ingredients:

- 2 cups Greek yogurt
- 1/4 cup honey
- 1/2 cup walnuts, chopped
- 1 teaspoon cinnamon (optional)

Instructions:

1. Divide Greek yogurt into serving bowls.
2. Drizzle honey over each portion and sprinkle with chopped walnuts. Add cinnamon if desired. Serve immediately.

Grilled Chicken with Tzatziki Sauce

Ingredients:

- 2 chicken breasts
- 2 tablespoons olive oil
- 1 teaspoon garlic powder
- 1 teaspoon oregano
- Salt and pepper to taste
- For the Tzatziki Sauce:
    - 1 cup Greek yogurt
    - 1 cucumber, grated and drained
    - 1 clove garlic, minced
    - 1 tablespoon olive oil
    - 1 tablespoon lemon juice
    - Salt to taste

Instructions:

1. Preheat the grill. In a bowl, mix olive oil, garlic powder, oregano, salt, and pepper. Coat chicken breasts with the mixture.
2. Grill chicken for 6-7 minutes on each side or until cooked through. Let rest before slicing.
3. For the tzatziki sauce, combine Greek yogurt, grated cucumber, garlic, olive oil, lemon juice, and salt in a bowl. Serve grilled chicken with tzatziki sauce on the side.

Roasted Red Pepper Hummus

Ingredients:

- 1 can (15 oz) chickpeas, drained and rinsed
- 1 roasted red pepper, chopped
- 1/4 cup tahini
- 2 tablespoons olive oil
- 2 tablespoons lemon juice
- 1 clove garlic
- Salt to taste

Instructions:

1. In a food processor, combine chickpeas, roasted red pepper, tahini, olive oil, lemon juice, garlic, and salt. Blend until smooth.
2. Add water as needed to reach desired consistency. Serve with pita bread or fresh vegetables.

Falafel with Tahini Sauce

Ingredients:

- 1 can (15 oz) chickpeas, drained and rinsed
- 1 small onion, chopped
- 2 cloves garlic, minced
- 1/4 cup fresh parsley, chopped
- 1 teaspoon cumin
- 1 teaspoon coriander
- Salt and pepper to taste
- Oil for frying
- For the Tahini Sauce:
    - 1/4 cup tahini
    - 2 tablespoons lemon juice
    - 2 tablespoons water
    - Salt to taste

Instructions:

1. In a food processor, combine chickpeas, onion, garlic, parsley, cumin, coriander, salt, and pepper. Blend until a coarse mixture forms.
2. Form into small balls and refrigerate for 30 minutes. Heat oil in a pan and fry falafel until golden brown on all sides.
3. For the tahini sauce, whisk together tahini, lemon juice, water, and salt. Serve falafel with tahini sauce.

Tomato and Cucumber Salad with Olive Oil

Ingredients:

- 2 cups cherry tomatoes, halved
- 1 cucumber, diced
- 1/2 red onion, thinly sliced
- 1/4 cup fresh basil, chopped
- 2 tablespoons olive oil
- 1 tablespoon red wine vinegar
- Salt and pepper to taste

Instructions:

1. In a large bowl, combine cherry tomatoes, cucumber, red onion, and basil.
2. Drizzle with olive oil and red wine vinegar. Season with salt and pepper. Toss to combine and serve chilled.

Shrimp Saganaki with Feta

Ingredients:

- 1 pound shrimp, peeled and deveined
- 1 cup diced tomatoes (fresh or canned)
- 1/2 cup feta cheese, crumbled
- 1/2 onion, chopped
- 2 cloves garlic, minced
- 1 teaspoon oregano
- 2 tablespoons olive oil
- Fresh parsley for garnish

Instructions:

1. In a skillet, heat olive oil over medium heat. Sauté onion and garlic until soft.
2. Add diced tomatoes and oregano, cooking for 5-7 minutes. Add shrimp and cook until pink and opaque.
3. Stir in feta cheese and cook for another minute until melted. Garnish with fresh parsley and serve warm.

Enjoy these delicious Greek dishes!

Grilled Zucchini with Lemon and Garlic

Ingredients:

- 2 medium zucchini, sliced into rounds
- 2 tablespoons olive oil
- 2 cloves garlic, minced
- 1 lemon, juiced
- Salt and pepper to taste
- Fresh parsley for garnish

Instructions:

1. Preheat the grill to medium-high heat.
2. In a bowl, combine olive oil, garlic, lemon juice, salt, and pepper. Add zucchini slices and toss to coat.
3. Grill zucchini for about 3-4 minutes on each side until tender and grill marks appear.
4. Remove from grill and garnish with fresh parsley before serving.

Whole Wheat Pita Bread with Olive Tapenade

Ingredients:

- **For the Pita Bread:**
    - 2 cups whole wheat flour
    - 1 packet (2 1/4 teaspoons) instant yeast
    - 1 teaspoon salt
    - 3/4 cup warm water
    - 1 tablespoon olive oil
- **For the Olive Tapenade:**
    - 1 cup mixed olives, pitted
    - 2 tablespoons capers
    - 1 garlic clove
    - 1 tablespoon olive oil
    - 1 tablespoon lemon juice

Instructions:

1. **For the Pita Bread:** In a bowl, combine flour, yeast, and salt. Add warm water and olive oil, mixing until a dough forms. Knead for 5 minutes. Cover and let rise for 1 hour.
2. Preheat the oven to 500°F (260°C) and place a baking sheet inside to heat.
3. Roll out dough into 1/4-inch thick rounds and place on the hot baking sheet. Bake for 5-7 minutes until puffed and golden.
4. **For the Olive Tapenade:** In a food processor, combine olives, capers, garlic, olive oil, and lemon juice. Blend until smooth. Serve with warm pita bread.

Lentil Soup with Lemon and Spinach

Ingredients:

- 1 cup lentils, rinsed
- 1 onion, chopped
- 2 carrots, diced
- 2 celery stalks, diced
- 2 cloves garlic, minced
- 6 cups vegetable broth
- 2 cups fresh spinach
- Juice of 1 lemon
- Salt and pepper to taste
- Olive oil for sautéing

Instructions:

1. In a large pot, heat olive oil over medium heat. Sauté onion, carrots, and celery until softened.
2. Add garlic and cook for 1 more minute. Stir in lentils and vegetable broth.
3. Bring to a boil, then reduce heat and simmer for 30-40 minutes until lentils are tender.
4. Stir in fresh spinach and lemon juice. Season with salt and pepper before serving.

Stuffed Grape Leaves (Dolmades)

Ingredients:

- 1 jar grape leaves, rinsed and drained
- 1 cup rice, rinsed
- 1 onion, finely chopped
- 1/2 cup pine nuts (optional)
- 1/2 cup fresh dill, chopped
- 1/2 cup fresh parsley, chopped
- Juice of 1 lemon
- Salt and pepper to taste
- 2 cups vegetable broth

Instructions:

1. In a skillet, sauté onion in olive oil until translucent. Add rice and cook for 2-3 minutes. Stir in pine nuts, dill, parsley, lemon juice, salt, and pepper.
2. Lay out grape leaves and place a spoonful of filling at the base. Roll tightly, tucking in the sides.
3. Place stuffed leaves seam-side down in a pot. Pour vegetable broth over them. Cover and simmer for 40-50 minutes until rice is cooked. Serve warm.

Couscous with Roasted Vegetables

Ingredients:

- 1 cup couscous
- 1 1/2 cups vegetable broth
- 2 cups mixed vegetables (zucchini, bell peppers, carrots, etc.), diced
- 2 tablespoons olive oil
- Salt and pepper to taste
- Fresh herbs (parsley or basil) for garnish

Instructions:

1. Preheat the oven to 400°F (200°C). Toss mixed vegetables with olive oil, salt, and pepper on a baking sheet. Roast for 20-25 minutes until tender.
2. In a pot, bring vegetable broth to a boil. Stir in couscous, remove from heat, and let sit for 5 minutes.
3. Fluff couscous with a fork and mix in roasted vegetables. Garnish with fresh herbs before serving.

Grilled Swordfish with Capers and Olive Oil

Ingredients:

- 2 swordfish steaks
- 2 tablespoons olive oil
- 2 tablespoons capers, drained
- Juice of 1 lemon
- Salt and pepper to taste

Instructions:

1. Preheat the grill to medium-high heat. Brush swordfish steaks with olive oil and season with salt and pepper.
2. Grill swordfish for about 5-6 minutes on each side until cooked through and flaky.
3. Drizzle with lemon juice and sprinkle capers over the top before serving.

Roasted Eggplant Dip (Baba Ganoush)

Ingredients:

- 1 large eggplant
- 1/4 cup tahini
- 2 tablespoons olive oil
- 2 tablespoons lemon juice
- 2 cloves garlic, minced
- Salt to taste
- Fresh parsley for garnish

Instructions:

1. Preheat the oven to 400°F (200°C). Pierce the eggplant with a fork and roast for 30-40 minutes until tender. Let cool.
2. Scoop out the flesh and combine it in a bowl with tahini, olive oil, lemon juice, garlic, and salt. Blend until smooth.
3. Serve garnished with fresh parsley and a drizzle of olive oil. Enjoy with pita bread or fresh vegetables.

These dishes celebrate the vibrant flavors of Mediterranean cuisine! Enjoy your cooking!

Chicken Souvlaki with Tzatziki

Ingredients:

- **For the Souvlaki:**
    - 1 pound chicken breast, cut into cubes
    - 2 tablespoons olive oil
    - Juice of 1 lemon
    - 2 cloves garlic, minced
    - 1 teaspoon dried oregano
    - Salt and pepper to taste
- **For the Tzatziki:**
    - 1 cup Greek yogurt
    - 1 cucumber, grated and drained
    - 1 clove garlic, minced
    - 1 tablespoon olive oil
    - 1 tablespoon fresh dill, chopped
    - Salt to taste

Instructions:

1. **For the Souvlaki:** In a bowl, combine olive oil, lemon juice, garlic, oregano, salt, and pepper. Add chicken cubes and marinate for at least 30 minutes.
2. Preheat the grill to medium-high heat. Thread marinated chicken onto skewers and grill for 10-12 minutes, turning occasionally until cooked through.
3. **For the Tzatziki:** In a bowl, mix together Greek yogurt, grated cucumber, garlic, olive oil, dill, and salt. Chill until ready to serve.
4. Serve chicken souvlaki with tzatziki sauce.

Roasted Cauliflower with Lemon and Garlic

Ingredients:

- 1 head cauliflower, cut into florets
- 3 tablespoons olive oil
- 4 cloves garlic, minced
- Juice of 1 lemon
- Salt and pepper to taste
- Fresh parsley for garnish

Instructions:

1. Preheat the oven to 425°F (220°C).
2. In a large bowl, toss cauliflower florets with olive oil, garlic, lemon juice, salt, and pepper.
3. Spread cauliflower on a baking sheet in a single layer. Roast for 25-30 minutes, flipping halfway, until golden brown and tender.
4. Garnish with fresh parsley before serving.

Mediterranean Tuna Salad

Ingredients:

- 2 cans tuna in olive oil, drained
- 1 cup cherry tomatoes, halved
- 1/2 cup red onion, finely chopped
- 1/2 cup Kalamata olives, pitted and chopped
- 1/4 cup fresh parsley, chopped
- 2 tablespoons capers, rinsed
- Juice of 1 lemon
- Salt and pepper to taste

Instructions:

1. In a large bowl, combine drained tuna, cherry tomatoes, red onion, olives, parsley, and capers.
2. Drizzle with lemon juice and season with salt and pepper. Toss gently to combine.
3. Serve chilled or at room temperature.

Chickpea and Spinach Stew

Ingredients:

- 1 can chickpeas, drained and rinsed
- 2 cups fresh spinach
- 1 onion, chopped
- 2 cloves garlic, minced
- 1 can diced tomatoes
- 1 teaspoon ground cumin
- 1 teaspoon paprika
- Salt and pepper to taste
- Olive oil for sautéing

Instructions:

1. In a large pot, heat olive oil over medium heat. Sauté onion until translucent, then add garlic and cook for another minute.
2. Stir in chickpeas, diced tomatoes, cumin, paprika, salt, and pepper. Simmer for 15 minutes.
3. Add spinach and cook until wilted. Adjust seasoning and serve hot.

Whole Wheat Pasta with Pesto and Tomatoes

Ingredients:

- 8 ounces whole wheat pasta
- 1 cup basil pesto
- 1 cup cherry tomatoes, halved
- 1/4 cup Parmesan cheese, grated
- Salt and pepper to taste
- Fresh basil for garnish

Instructions:

1. Cook pasta according to package instructions. Drain and set aside.
2. In a large bowl, combine cooked pasta, pesto, and cherry tomatoes. Toss to coat.
3. Season with salt and pepper, and sprinkle with Parmesan cheese and fresh basil before serving.

Grilled Halloumi Cheese with Tomato

Ingredients:

- 8 ounces halloumi cheese, sliced
- 2 large tomatoes, sliced
- 2 tablespoons olive oil
- Fresh basil leaves for garnish
- Salt and pepper to taste

Instructions:

1. Preheat the grill to medium-high heat.
2. Brush halloumi slices with olive oil and grill for about 2-3 minutes on each side until golden brown.
3. On a platter, layer grilled halloumi and tomato slices. Drizzle with olive oil, and season with salt and pepper.
4. Garnish with fresh basil leaves before serving.

Braised Artichokes with Garlic and Herbs

Ingredients:

- 4 fresh artichokes, trimmed
- 3 tablespoons olive oil
- 4 cloves garlic, sliced
- 1 lemon, juiced
- 1 cup vegetable broth
- Fresh herbs (thyme, parsley) for garnish

Instructions:

1. In a large pot, heat olive oil over medium heat. Add garlic and sauté until fragrant.
2. Place trimmed artichokes cut side down in the pot. Add lemon juice and vegetable broth. Bring to a simmer, cover, and cook for 30-40 minutes until tender.
3. Garnish with fresh herbs before serving.

These Mediterranean dishes are packed with flavor and make for delicious and healthy meals! Enjoy your cooking!

Caprese Salad with Fresh Mozzarella

Ingredients:

- 4 ripe tomatoes, sliced
- 8 ounces fresh mozzarella cheese, sliced
- Fresh basil leaves
- 3 tablespoons extra virgin olive oil
- Balsamic glaze (optional)
- Salt and pepper to taste

Instructions:

1. On a large plate, alternate slices of tomatoes and mozzarella.
2. Tuck fresh basil leaves between the layers.
3. Drizzle with olive oil and balsamic glaze, if using. Season with salt and pepper before serving.

Sardines with Lemon and Olive Oil

Ingredients:

- 2 cans sardines in olive oil, drained
- 2 tablespoons fresh lemon juice
- 1 tablespoon chopped fresh parsley
- Lemon wedges for serving
- Salt and pepper to taste

Instructions:

1. Arrange sardines on a plate. Drizzle with lemon juice and olive oil.
2. Sprinkle with chopped parsley, salt, and pepper.
3. Serve with lemon wedges.

Roasted Beet Salad with Feta

Ingredients:

- 4 medium beets, roasted and sliced
- 4 ounces feta cheese, crumbled
- 2 cups arugula or mixed greens
- 1/4 cup walnuts, toasted
- 3 tablespoons balsamic vinegar
- 2 tablespoons olive oil
- Salt and pepper to taste

Instructions:

1. In a large bowl, combine roasted beet slices, arugula, and walnuts.
2. Drizzle with balsamic vinegar and olive oil. Toss gently to combine.
3. Top with crumbled feta and season with salt and pepper before serving.

Grilled Octopus with Olive Oil and Herbs

Ingredients:

- 2 pounds octopus, cleaned
- 1/4 cup olive oil
- 4 cloves garlic, minced
- 1 tablespoon fresh oregano, chopped
- Juice of 1 lemon
- Salt and pepper to taste

Instructions:

1. Boil octopus in salted water for 30-40 minutes until tender. Drain and cool.
2. Preheat the grill to medium-high heat. Cut octopus into tentacles and brush with olive oil, garlic, oregano, salt, and pepper.
3. Grill for 3-4 minutes on each side until charred. Drizzle with lemon juice before serving.

Lemon Orzo Salad with Feta and Olives

Ingredients:

- 1 cup orzo pasta
- 1 cup cherry tomatoes, halved
- 1/2 cup Kalamata olives, pitted and sliced
- 1/2 cup feta cheese, crumbled
- 1/4 cup fresh parsley, chopped
- Juice of 1 lemon
- 2 tablespoons olive oil
- Salt and pepper to taste

Instructions:

1. Cook orzo according to package instructions. Drain and let cool.
2. In a large bowl, combine cooked orzo, cherry tomatoes, olives, feta, and parsley.
3. Drizzle with lemon juice and olive oil. Season with salt and pepper, then toss to combine.

Roasted Bell Peppers with Anchovies

Ingredients:

- 4 bell peppers (red, yellow, or orange), halved and seeded
- 1 can anchovies, drained
- 3 tablespoons olive oil
- 2 cloves garlic, minced
- Fresh parsley for garnish
- Salt and pepper to taste

Instructions:

1. Preheat the oven to 400°F (200°C). Place bell pepper halves on a baking sheet.
2. In a bowl, mix anchovies, olive oil, garlic, salt, and pepper. Spoon mixture into the bell pepper halves.
3. Roast for 25-30 minutes until peppers are tender. Garnish with fresh parsley before serving.

Ratatouille with Fresh Herbs

Ingredients:

- 1 eggplant, diced
- 2 zucchinis, diced
- 1 bell pepper, diced
- 1 onion, chopped
- 3 cloves garlic, minced
- 1 can diced tomatoes
- 1 teaspoon dried thyme
- 1 teaspoon dried basil
- Fresh basil for garnish
- Olive oil, salt, and pepper to taste

Instructions:

1. In a large pot, heat olive oil over medium heat. Add onion and garlic, cooking until softened.
2. Stir in eggplant, zucchini, and bell pepper. Cook for about 5-7 minutes.
3. Add diced tomatoes, thyme, basil, salt, and pepper. Simmer for 20-25 minutes until vegetables are tender.
4. Garnish with fresh basil before serving.

Enjoy these delightful Mediterranean dishes that highlight fresh ingredients and vibrant flavors!

Bulgur Wheat Salad with Pomegranate Seeds

Ingredients:

- 1 cup bulgur wheat
- 2 cups boiling water
- 1 cup pomegranate seeds
- 1/2 cup cucumber, diced
- 1/4 cup red onion, finely chopped
- 1/4 cup parsley, chopped
- 3 tablespoons olive oil
- 2 tablespoons lemon juice
- Salt and pepper to taste

Instructions:

1. In a large bowl, combine bulgur wheat and boiling water. Cover and let it sit for 15-20 minutes until the water is absorbed.
2. Fluff the bulgur with a fork and add pomegranate seeds, cucumber, red onion, and parsley.
3. Drizzle with olive oil and lemon juice. Season with salt and pepper before serving.

Baked Cod with Tomatoes and Olives

Ingredients:

- 4 cod fillets
- 2 cups cherry tomatoes, halved
- 1/2 cup Kalamata olives, pitted and halved
- 3 tablespoons olive oil
- 2 cloves garlic, minced
- 1 teaspoon dried oregano
- Salt and pepper to taste

Instructions:

1. Preheat the oven to 400°F (200°C). Arrange cod fillets in a baking dish.
2. In a bowl, combine cherry tomatoes, olives, olive oil, garlic, oregano, salt, and pepper. Mix well.
3. Pour the tomato-olive mixture over the cod fillets. Bake for 20-25 minutes until the fish is cooked through.

Greek Lentil Salad with Red Wine Vinegar

Ingredients:

- 1 cup lentils, rinsed and drained
- 1/4 cup red onion, finely chopped
- 1/2 cup cucumber, diced
- 1/2 cup cherry tomatoes, halved
- 1/4 cup feta cheese, crumbled
- 3 tablespoons red wine vinegar
- 2 tablespoons olive oil
- Salt and pepper to taste

Instructions:

1. Cook lentils in a pot of boiling water for 20-25 minutes until tender. Drain and let cool.
2. In a large bowl, combine cooked lentils, red onion, cucumber, tomatoes, and feta cheese.
3. Drizzle with red wine vinegar and olive oil. Season with salt and pepper before tossing gently to combine.

Zucchini Fritters with Feta

Ingredients:

- 2 medium zucchinis, grated
- 1/2 cup feta cheese, crumbled
- 1/4 cup all-purpose flour
- 2 eggs, beaten
- 2 cloves garlic, minced
- Salt and pepper to taste
- Olive oil for frying

Instructions:

1. In a bowl, combine grated zucchini, feta cheese, flour, eggs, garlic, salt, and pepper. Mix well.
2. Heat olive oil in a skillet over medium heat. Drop spoonfuls of the mixture into the pan and flatten slightly.
3. Cook for 3-4 minutes on each side until golden brown. Drain on paper towels before serving.

Roasted Garlic and Herb Chicken

Ingredients:

- 4 chicken breasts
- 1 head garlic, roasted
- 2 tablespoons olive oil
- 1 tablespoon fresh rosemary, chopped
- 1 tablespoon fresh thyme, chopped
- Salt and pepper to taste

Instructions:

1. Preheat the oven to 375°F (190°C). In a bowl, mix roasted garlic, olive oil, rosemary, thyme, salt, and pepper to create a paste.
2. Rub the paste over chicken breasts and place them in a baking dish.
3. Bake for 25-30 minutes until the chicken is cooked through and juices run clear.

Cucumber Yogurt Soup

Ingredients:

- 2 cups plain yogurt
- 1 cucumber, peeled and diced
- 1/4 cup fresh dill, chopped
- 2 cloves garlic, minced
- 1 tablespoon lemon juice
- Salt and pepper to taste

Instructions:

1. In a bowl, combine yogurt, cucumber, dill, garlic, lemon juice, salt, and pepper. Mix until well combined.
2. Chill in the refrigerator for at least 30 minutes before serving.

Baked Falafel with Tzatziki

Ingredients:

- 1 can chickpeas, drained and rinsed
- 1/4 cup parsley, chopped
- 1/4 cup onion, chopped
- 2 cloves garlic, minced
- 1 teaspoon cumin
- 1 teaspoon coriander
- 1/2 cup breadcrumbs
- Salt and pepper to taste
- Olive oil for brushing

Instructions:

1. Preheat the oven to 375°F (190°C). In a food processor, combine chickpeas, parsley, onion, garlic, cumin, coriander, breadcrumbs, salt, and pepper. Pulse until combined.
2. Shape the mixture into small balls and place on a baking sheet lined with parchment paper. Brush with olive oil.
3. Bake for 25-30 minutes until golden brown. Serve with tzatziki sauce.

Enjoy these delicious Mediterranean-inspired dishes that bring vibrant flavors to your table!

Olive Oil and Lemon Marinated Artichokes

Ingredients:

- 1 can artichoke hearts, drained and halved
- 1/4 cup olive oil
- 2 tablespoons lemon juice
- 2 cloves garlic, minced
- 1 teaspoon dried oregano
- Salt and pepper to taste
- Fresh parsley, chopped (for garnish)

Instructions:

1. In a bowl, whisk together olive oil, lemon juice, garlic, oregano, salt, and pepper.
2. Add the artichoke hearts to the bowl and toss to coat. Let marinate for at least 30 minutes.
3. Serve chilled or at room temperature, garnished with fresh parsley.

Grilled Vegetable Skewers with Halloumi

Ingredients:

- 1 zucchini, sliced
- 1 bell pepper, chopped
- 1 red onion, chopped
- 1 cup cherry tomatoes
- 8 oz halloumi cheese, cut into cubes
- 2 tablespoons olive oil
- 1 teaspoon dried oregano
- Salt and pepper to taste

Instructions:

1. Preheat the grill to medium-high heat. In a bowl, toss the vegetables and halloumi with olive oil, oregano, salt, and pepper.
2. Thread the vegetables and halloumi onto skewers.
3. Grill skewers for 8-10 minutes, turning occasionally, until vegetables are tender and halloumi is golden brown.

Mediterranean Stuffed Eggplant

Ingredients:

- 2 medium eggplants, halved
- 1 cup cooked quinoa
- 1 cup diced tomatoes
- 1/2 cup chickpeas, rinsed and drained
- 1/4 cup feta cheese, crumbled
- 2 tablespoons olive oil
- 1 teaspoon dried basil
- Salt and pepper to taste

Instructions:

1. Preheat the oven to 375°F (190°C). Scoop out the flesh of the eggplants, leaving a 1/2-inch border.
2. In a bowl, mix quinoa, tomatoes, chickpeas, feta, olive oil, basil, salt, and pepper.
3. Fill the eggplant halves with the mixture and place on a baking sheet. Bake for 25-30 minutes until eggplant is tender.

Tomato and Feta Salad with Fresh Herbs

Ingredients:

- 4 cups cherry tomatoes, halved
- 1/2 cup feta cheese, crumbled
- 1/4 cup red onion, thinly sliced
- 2 tablespoons fresh basil, chopped
- 2 tablespoons fresh parsley, chopped
- 3 tablespoons olive oil
- 1 tablespoon balsamic vinegar
- Salt and pepper to taste

Instructions:

1. In a large bowl, combine cherry tomatoes, feta, red onion, basil, and parsley.
2. Drizzle with olive oil and balsamic vinegar. Season with salt and pepper, then toss gently to combine.

Baked Sea Bass with Lemon and Capers

Ingredients:

- 4 sea bass fillets
- 2 tablespoons olive oil
- 2 tablespoons capers, rinsed and drained
- 1 lemon, sliced
- Salt and pepper to taste
- Fresh parsley, for garnish

Instructions:

1. Preheat the oven to 400°F (200°C). Place sea bass fillets in a baking dish.
2. Drizzle with olive oil, and top with capers and lemon slices. Season with salt and pepper.
3. Bake for 15-20 minutes until the fish is cooked through. Garnish with fresh parsley before serving.

Quinoa and Avocado Salad with Olive Oil

Ingredients:

- 1 cup cooked quinoa
- 1 ripe avocado, diced
- 1 cup cherry tomatoes, halved
- 1/4 cup red onion, finely chopped
- 2 tablespoons olive oil
- 1 tablespoon lime juice
- Salt and pepper to taste

Instructions:

1. In a large bowl, combine quinoa, avocado, cherry tomatoes, and red onion.
2. Drizzle with olive oil and lime juice. Season with salt and pepper, and toss gently to combine.

Spinach Salad with Feta and Walnuts

Ingredients:

- 4 cups fresh spinach, washed and dried
- 1/2 cup feta cheese, crumbled
- 1/2 cup walnuts, toasted
- 1/4 cup red onion, thinly sliced
- 3 tablespoons olive oil
- 1 tablespoon balsamic vinegar
- Salt and pepper to taste

Instructions:

1. In a large bowl, combine spinach, feta, walnuts, and red onion.
2. Drizzle with olive oil and balsamic vinegar. Season with salt and pepper, and toss to combine.

Mediterranean Lentil Soup

Ingredients:

- 1 cup lentils, rinsed and drained
- 1 onion, chopped
- 2 carrots, chopped
- 2 celery stalks, chopped
- 3 cloves garlic, minced
- 4 cups vegetable broth
- 1 can diced tomatoes
- 1 teaspoon cumin
- 1 teaspoon smoked paprika
- Salt and pepper to taste

Instructions:

1. In a large pot, sauté onion, carrots, and celery in olive oil until softened.
2. Add garlic, lentils, vegetable broth, diced tomatoes, cumin, smoked paprika, salt, and pepper.
3. Bring to a boil, then reduce heat and simmer for 30-40 minutes until lentils are tender.

These Mediterranean recipes are flavorful, healthy, and perfect for any meal! Enjoy!

www.ingramcontent.com/pod-product-compliance
Lightning Source LLC
LaVergne TN
LVHW081342060526
838201LV00055B/2794